ADVENTUROUS SEX

RANDI FOXX

ADVENTUROUS

SEX

EROTIC EXPLOITS FOR DARING COUPLES

CARLTON
BOOKS

THIS IS A CARLTON BOOK

This edition published by
Carlton Books Limited 2007
20 Mortimer Street
London W1T 3JW

Copyright © Hylas Publishing 2004
The moral right of the author has been asserted.

First published in 2004 by Hylas Publishing
129 Main Street, Suite C
Irvington, New York, 10533
www.hylaspublishing.com

ISBN-10: 1-84442-077-9
ISBN-13: 978-1-84442-077-3

Printed and bound in Singapore

Contents

Bed Action

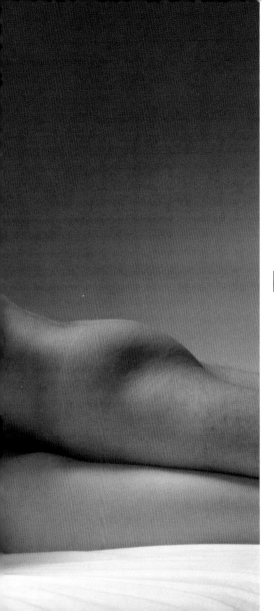

1

Straight-Edge Sex A

Most commonly known as the Missionary Position; also called the Clasping position. The man is on top and the legs of both the man and woman are stretched out straight. Both partners face one another.

2

Foot Rub with Rhythm

In Straight-Edge Sex A (1), the man turns a full 360° while in union. When he is 180° to his partner, he can stop to give her a nice foot massage! (She can take this opportunity to caress his buttocks and get a new view of her lover's body). It takes a lot of practice to do this move without the penis slipping out repeatedly, but the angles of penetration are worth it!

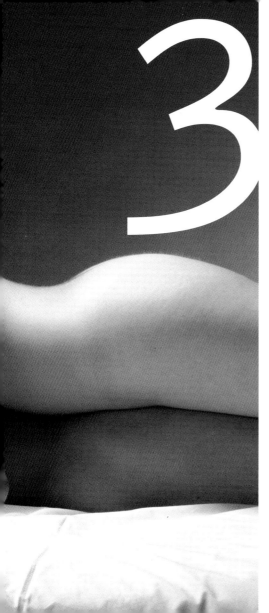

3

Straight-Edge Sex B

Straight-Edge Sex A (1), but with the woman on top.

4

Always by Your Side

Variation of Straight-Edge Sex, with both partners face to face, but on their sides. A hand is then free to explore the rest of your lover's body.

17

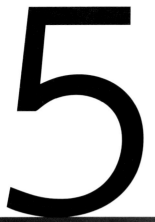

5 Pig in a Blanket

The most natural progression from Straight-Edge Sex A (1) While the man is on top, the woman wraps her legs around his waist, pulling him into her more.

6

The Penitent Forgiven

A slight shift from the Pig in a Blanket (5); the legs of the woman are still wrapped around the man (who is on top), but the man is kneeling with his arms at her sides.

21

7

The Awakening

Also known as the "Yawning position," but hardly boring. A natural progression from Penitent Forgiven (6). The woman, whose thighs are wrapped around her lover, raises her legs and keeps them apart in the air, allowing for full penetration.

8

The Piked Awakening

Acrobatic variation of the Awakening (7); the woman throws her raised legs back in a pike position and lifts her vagina, allowing for full and deep penetration. For better control, she can hold her calves with her hands. (A pillow under her lower back also helps). The man, who is on top, relies mostly on upper-body strength and can lie or kneel over the woman.

Inner Awakening

Variation of Awakening (7), with the legs of the woman on the inside of the man's arms, allowing her to rest her legs on his shoulders, or to bend them back over his arms. This position is more comfortable for the woman than the Awakening, and can be sustained for longer. She also has better access to his buttocks and face.

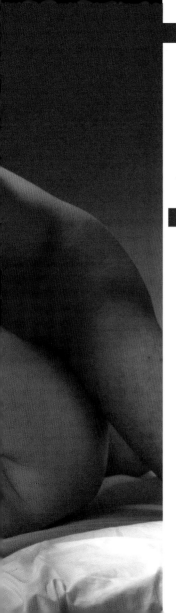

10

Scissors

Similar to Splitting of a Bamboo
(11); while on her back, the
woman moves her legs back and
forth in the air while penetrated
by her kneeling lover. This motion
squeezes the penis, causing powerful sensations for both partners.

11

Splitting of a Bamboo

Straight from the **Kama Sutra**—an easy progression from the Inner Awakening (9). The woman uses the motion of her legs to squeeze the penis while it is in the vagina. A single leg rises onto her partner's shoulder and then lowers; the other leg repeats this motion.

12

Hammerhead

Variation of Splitting of a Bamboo (11); the act is similar to hammering in a nail—while the man kneels and thrusts forward, the woman places her foot on his forehead instead of on his shoulder.

13

Jackknifed Splits

Similar to Splitting of a Bamboo (11), but the woman has one leg under her kneeling lover and the other raised across his body, resting against his face. From this vantage point, the man can see his penis thrust in and out of the vagina, and the woman's breasts undulate in rhythm to the motion.

14

Lateral Jackknifed Splits

In a natural move from Jackknifed Splits (13), the woman's leg comes over the side of her partner, resting against his thigh. This position is the perfect prelude to the Elephant (74).

15

Climbing Ivy

The man kneels while facing his lover, who lies on her back. She raises her legs and wraps them around his neck, allowing for deep penetration. He can take hold of her thighs and guide himself into her.

16

Inverted Wheelbarrow

An extreme variation of Climbing Ivy (15); the woman is almost upside-down, with only her head and neck on the bed. Her legs are on either side of her lover's head, and her lower back and buttocks are in the air. She may want to hold onto his thighs for support, and he will have to hold her legs while inside of her.

17

The Crab

Moving from the Awakening (7), the man takes a more dominating role and the woman pulls herself into a ball, with her legs folded against her chest. The man straddles her while kneeling, allowing for deep penetration.

18

The Wrapped Crab

The man crouches on the balls of his feet, and the woman, on her back, moves from the Crab (17) and wraps her legs over his thighs.

19

The Open Crab

Instead of pushing the folded legs
against her chest, the woman
opens her legs and rests her feet
on her lover's thighs. Her vagina is
fully open and her breasts are also
exposed. The man is in control and
can add to his dominance by pushing down on her shoulders.

20

The Press

The woman is on her back and presses her feet against her partner's chest. He faces her while sitting up on his back legs, allowing for deep penetration.

21

The Bicycle

Similar to Splitting of a Bamboo (11); the woman presses one foot against her lover's chest and raises the other leg in the air, as though she were riding a bicycle.

22

Side-to-Side Press

Variation of the Press (20); the man takes
his lover's ankles, removes them from his
chest, and shifts them from one side of his
body to the other. This motion causes her
vaginal muscles to contract around the
penis. At the same time, he can kiss and
caress her legs, ankles, and feet.

Half Lotus

Natural progression from the Crab (17); the man leans
forward and supports his lover's body. When she pulls her legs
up, she crosses her shins while pressing her thighs against her chest.

23

24

Full Lotus

Takes the lotus position of yoga and brings it into
the bedroom. The woman assumes this position
while on her back with her legs folded above her.
Her partner leans forward and enters her while
facing her and resting back on his legs.

58

25

Wife of Indra

Extreme variation of the Crab (17); the woman pushes her legs back and to her sides instead of letting them rest against her chest. This position fully opens the vagina to the man for deep penetration.

Kneel and Extend

The woman lies on her back and pulls in her knees. The man kneels in front of her and enters her. She then extends both legs to one of his shoulders. This position allows him to caress her thighs.

27

Lateral Kneel and Extend

Instead of raising her legs to her lover's shoulder, while on her back, the woman drapes her legs over one of his thighs. The man sits back on his legs and faces her. From this vantage point, he can see her getting aroused and may stroke her clitoris and breasts.

28

Kneel and Push Back

Variation of the Kneel and Extend (26); instead of letting her legs rest on his shoulder, the man holds them away from him, altering the angle of penetration.

Side-to-Side Kneel and Extend

Variation of the Lateral Kneel and Extend (27); the woman swivels her legs back and forth from one of her lover's thighs to the other. This angle works well for G-spot arousal.

9

30

Surf's Up

The woman lies on her back with her legs extended above her. The man lies across her, preparing to catch the next wave of pleasure.

31

The Pelvic Thrust

From Straight-Edge Sex A (1), the woman moves her legs apart so that they are on the outside of the man's legs. The woman lowers her head, and raises her pelvis toward her partner. In this position, the vagina is fully open, allowing for deep penetration.

Pelvic Lap Dance

While on her back, the woman places her feet down and thrusts her pelvis up toward the man who is sitting on his hind legs. Similar to the Pelvic Thrust (31) with one important difference: the woman's buttocks are resting on her lover's thighs. While the woman arches her back, the man has full access to her stomach and breasts.

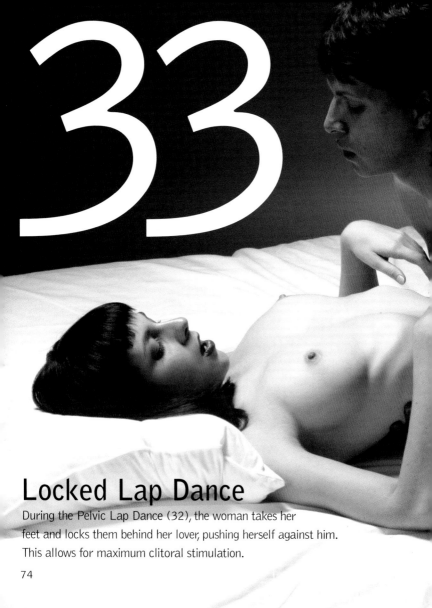

33

Locked Lap Dance

During the Pelvic Lap Dance (32), the woman takes her
feet and locks them behind her lover, pushing herself against him.
This allows for maximum clitoral stimulation.

74

34

Kama's Wheel

Both partners sit facing one another, with
the woman on the man's lap. The man sits
with his legs outstretched and his lover mirrors
his position (thus creating the spokes of a
wheel with their legs).

35

Reclining Kama's Wheel

While in the Kama's Wheel (34), the woman leans back on her elbows, altering the angle of penetration. Her legs wrap around the back of her partner.

3

Snake Trap

While in the Kama's Wheel (34), the woman leans
back and grasps her partner's ankles. She uses her
pelvic muscles to grip her lover's penis and rock gently
back and forth.

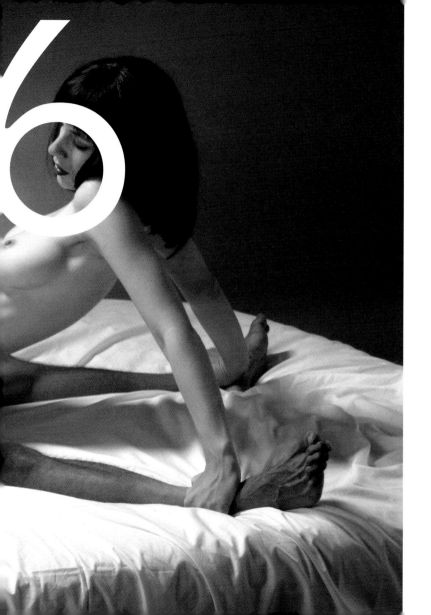

37

Full Reclining Snake Trap

Both lovers lean back while in the Kama's Wheel (34), forcing
the woman to use her vaginal muscles to maintain his erection.
The couple focuses on stimulating their subtle energy bodies
rather than their physical bodies—very tantric!

38

The Neverending Hug

The lovers sit face to face, straddling each other's
bodies. A position that allows for deep penetration,
kissing, and eye contact.

39

Paired Feet

From the Kama's Wheel (34), the woman leans back and draws her legs up so that her shins are resting on her partner's chest. The man opens his legs wide apart, with her body between them, so that the woman can experience full penetration. Then he presses her thighs together to intensify the sensations.

40

"X" Marks the Spot

Combination of the Full Reclining Snake Trap (37) and the Jackknifed Splits (13); the woman lies on her side with her legs apart. The man lies back with his legs apart. They meet in the middle, with one of her legs underneath him and her feet beside his face if he lies back.

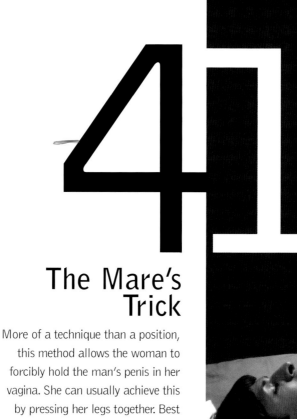

41

The Mare's Trick

More of a technique than a position, this method allows the woman to forcibly hold the man's penis in her vagina. She can usually achieve this by pressing her legs together. Best during Straight-Edge Sex B (3), where the woman is on top and can better control the action.

42

Pair of Tongs

Similar to the Mare's Trick (41); it is more of a sexual technique than a position. Once again, the woman straddles the man who is facing her while lying on his back. The woman holds the penis in her vagina—drawing it in, pressing it and keeping it in for a long time. Intense eye contact, and the woman stroking her lover's chest and testicles enhance this technique.

43

The Spinner

From the Bucking Bronco (51), the woman rotates 360°, experiencing every angle of penetration. She has the potential for G-spot activation while her back is to her lover. Perfect for smaller women with larger partners.

44

Back to Meditating

As the man lies on his back, his partner sits on him cross-legged with her back to him. Although there is little eye contact, the angle of entry is perfect for G-spot activation.

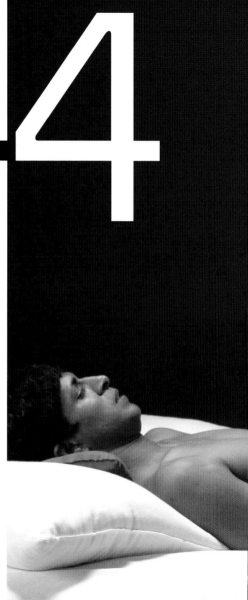

4

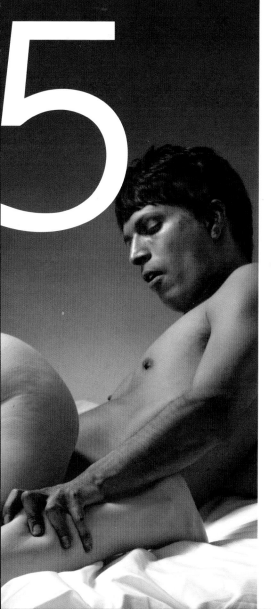

The Pin

The counterpart to Foot Rub with Rhythm (2); from Straight-Edge Sex B (3), the woman turns 180° and has her body between his legs while she rests on her hands (he is still on his back). Her legs straddle his.

Spoon-on-Spoon

Variation on part of the Spinner sequence (43);
while the woman has her back to the man, she lies
on top of him. This allows him to run his hands all
over her body, concentrating on her clitoris.

47

Stretched
Spoon-on-Spoon

From the Spoon-on-Spoon (46), the woman bends her legs back, increasing the angle of penetration and the opportunity for clitoral stimulation.

48

Sliding Into Home

Variation of the Bucking Bronco (51); the man's knees are bent so that the woman slides into him while on top of him. She can lean back onto his thighs as she rides him, leaving one hand free.

49

The Recliner

Another variation of the Bucking Bronco (51); while sitting
and facing the man, the woman leans back onto her elbows.
Her back is arched and he has full access to her clitoris. In this
position, she can push his penis against the wall of her vagina.

50

The Wrap Around

A shift from Sliding Into Home (48); the woman
has her back to her lover and wraps her arms
around his thighs as she sits straddles him.

51

The Bucking Bronco

The man lies on his back while the woman straddles her lover, facing him. She sits on him and rides him back and forth, and can place her hands on his chest while doing so. He has full access to her breasts and both partners can stimulate the clitoris.

52

Will You Do Me?

The man kneels on one bended knee as
though he were going to propose and
enters his partner who faces him while
kneeling with her legs apart.

53

Crouching Tiger, Hidden Passion

Both partners rest on the balls of their feet. Similar to Let Us Pray (54); the man is between his lover's legs. She places her arms around his neck for better support and he guides her in with his hands on her waist.

54

Let Us Pray

Both partners are on their
knees, sitting back on their
legs, facing one another. He is
between her legs and can hold
her for better control.

55

The Body Hug

A sitting position, where the man sits cross-legged and his partner sits in his lap facing him. She straddles him and wraps her legs around his back. This position allows the bodies to rub against each other fully and sensually.

56

Flexed Body Hug

While in the Body Hug (55), the woman raises her leg, and hangs it over her lover's arm. This alters the angle of penetration and tension between the vagina and penis.

57

Reclining Body Hug

While in the Body Hug
(55), the woman leans
back onto her elbows,
changing the angle of
penetration and exposing
her breasts for fondling.

58

Crying Out

From Paired Feet (39), the man slips his arms under his partner's knees and puts his hands on her waist to lift her. If there is too much strain on him, the woman can lean back and support some of her weight on her arms. The man then raises her and moves her from left to right to intensify the experience.

5

9

Sweet Abandon

The woman leans back onto her elbows, with her legs clasped behind her lover as she sits facing him.

60

The Corkscrew

While sitting up with his legs apart, knees bent and hands behind his back, the man welcomes his partner, who sits on his penis with her legs wrapped around his waist.

61

The Flexed Corkscrew

Variation on the Corkscrew (60); the woman's legs rest on her partner's shoulders instead of wrapping around his waist.

62

Inverted Headlock

The woman, on her back, faces her lover, who sits up while he straddles her. She raises her legs to either side of his head and locks her ankles behind his neck.

63

The See-Saw A

The man kneels and leans back on his legs, putting his arms behind him. His lover straddles him and rests her weight on the balls of her feet. She then rocks back and forth while on top.

64

The See-Saw B

While in See-Saw A (63), the woman turns from facing her lover and continues with her back to him.

65

The Backbend A

Also called the Swing, the man does a
backbend and maintains this position while
the woman mounts and rides him.

66

The Throne

The man lies back on the bed or on the floor and bends his knees above him. His partner sits on the back of his thighs, which form a sort of throne, and she mounts him in this fashion. Difficult to maintain, but worth the effort!

Back Door Policy

See Spot Come

The perennial doggy-style. The woman kneels on all fours and her partner kneels upright behind her, thrusting from that position. Her legs straddle his. This position allows for maximum G-spot activation.

68

The Dutch Doggy

Variation of See Spot Come (67); requires athleticism and some well-placed pillows. The woman, while being penetrated from behind, stretches out one leg, then the other in a windmill motion under her lover. This position allows for intense angles of penetration.

69

Taking Sides

Variation of See Spot Come (67) that allows the man to sit instead of kneel. The woman reclines with her back to her lover, partially resting on her side and supporting herself with her elbow. (A large pillow or cushion also helps to support her body). In this position, the woman does all of the work, sliding her pelvis back and forth to intensify the experience.

70

The Back Scratcher

The woman kneels on all fours in front of her lover; he kneels behind her and enters her from behind. She lifts a leg up and scratches his back with her foot.

71

Enveloped in Love

In an inverted Press (20), the woman lies on her stomach with her legs tucked under her and the man kneels over her, entering her from behind. Her exposed back is a sensitive area that will welcome the man's gentle caresses and warm chest.

72

Baby Elephant

Prelude to the Elephant (74); both partners are on their sides, supporting themselves with one arm. The man is stretched fully behind the woman and penetrates her from this position, which frees up his other hands for breast and clitoral stimulation.

Open Elephant

While in the Baby Elephant (72), the woman opens her leg, allowing for better clitoral stimulation.

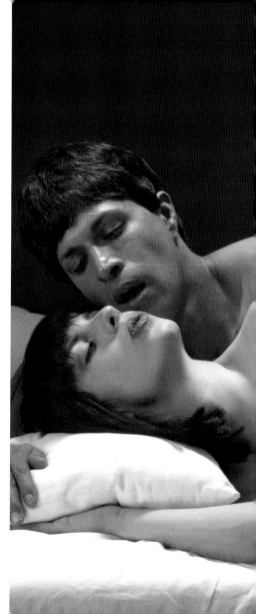

73

74

The Elephant

The woman lies on her stomach and the man lies on top of her, full body. His legs lie straight between hers and he penetrates her from behind, forgoing kissing and eye contact, but increasing G-spot activation angles and deep penetration.

On The Edge

75

Sitting Body Wrap

The man sits on the edge of the bed or in a backless chair; his partner sits on his lap facing him and wraps her legs around his back.

76

Sitting Flexed Body Wrap

While in the Sitting Body Wrap (75), the woman hangs her legs over her lover's arms, allowing for even closer contact and better clitoral stimulation.

The Backbend B

While in the Sitting Body Wrap (75), the woman does a backbend, easing her hands behind her so that her palms rest on the floor.

78

The Pushover

The woman's legs wrap around the waist of her lover, and she leans forward over his lap and places her hands on the floor. Perfect prelude to the Hoover (87).

79

The Cobra

From the Pushover (78), the woman raises her torso and rests her hands on the knees of her seated lover.

80

The Pilot

Instead of being a Pushover (78), the woman extends her legs back and her arms to her sides, assuming an airplane position while on her lover's lap.

The Standing O

81

The Stick Up

From the Tango (83), the woman
turns to have her back to her lover
and lifts one knee up, which the man
can hold in place. He then has access
to enter her from behind.

82

Stand by Your Man

The woman stands in front of her lover with her back to him. She straddles him, bending one leg behind his back. She may need to hold onto him for balance.

83

The Tango

Both partners stand and face each other. The woman wraps her arms around her lover's neck and one leg around his for leverage.

84

The Harness

The man stands with his feet shoulder-width apart. He holds his partner as she wraps her legs around his waist. This position requires strong upper-body strength for the man.

85

The Backbend C

While in the Harness (84), the woman eases herself back and tries to touch the floor with her
hands. Her legs are still locked behind her lover's
back for control and his arms must be strong to
support her weight. To reduce the strain on both
partners, try it off of the bed instead.

Congress of the Cow

The woman stands on the ground and places her palms flat in front of her, (or on the bed or a chair if she is not flexible enough). The man enters her from behind, and has full access to her buttocks in this powerful sexual stance. If the woman begins to feels lightheaded, move into the Stick Up (81).

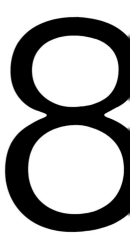

87

The Hoover

The woman rests her forearms on the floor
while her partner lifts the rest of her body
waist-level and enters her from behind. She
can clasp her legs around her lover's waist
for better control.

88

The Hoover Upright

The Hoover (87), but with the woman's feet clasped behind her lover's neck.

89

The Handstand

The Hoover Upright (88), but a little higher. The woman shifts her weight to her palms instead of resting on her forearms.

90

The Leg Up

Both lovers face each other while standing. The woman drapes her left leg over her partner's thigh and grabs on to allow for deep penetration.

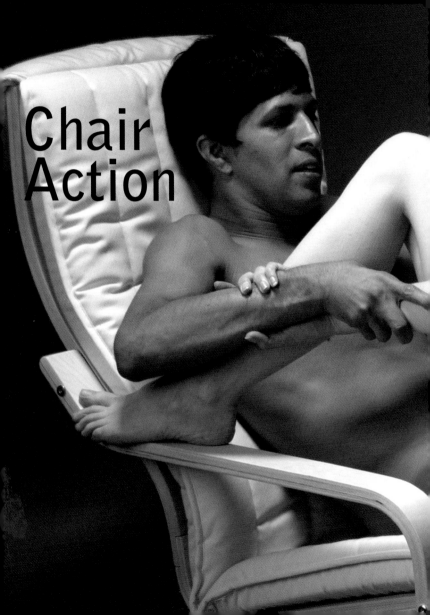

Chair
Action

198

91

The Chair Lift

With the help of a chair and a cushion, this kneeling position allows for deep penetration and new angles. The woman leans on the chair sideways, while her lover kneels in front of her. She can drape a leg over his thigh, allowing for clitoral stimulation.

92

Purrfect Plunge

The Cat position; similar to See Spot Come (67) without the woman as prostrate. The woman kneels upright and leans over a bed or rests against a chair while her lover enters her from behind. The woman's legs remain in between his, and her vertical posture allows for the fondling of her breasts and clitoris.

93

The Lounge Cat

While assuming the Purrfect Plunge
(92) on a chair, the woman is ready
for her lover to stand and enter her
from behind.

94

Fido's on His Feet

Doggy-style off the bed. The woman is on all fours or simply kneeling on a chair, and the man stands behind her, mounting her from this position.

95

The Wheelbarrow

The Hoover (87) for your bed or chair. Same concept, except that the woman has a cushiony support for her forearms, and the angle is not as extreme.

96

Lay-Z Girl

The woman sits in a large easy chair
and the man kneels in front of her.
She wraps her legs around his back.
Easy on both partners, as no one has
to support the other's weight.

97

Tug of War

While sitting in a chair, the man slides forward so that only his shoulders and head are resting against the back of the chair. His lover mounts him, resting her feet against the lower back or on the arms of the chair while holding onto his hands.

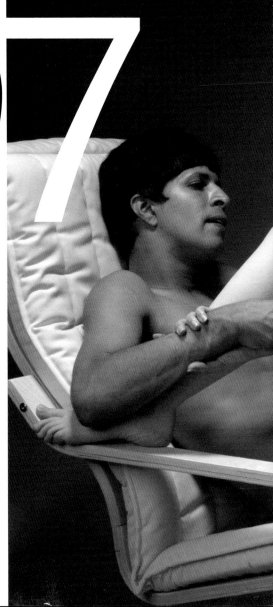

98

Come Sit on My Lap

The man sits or lies on a chair and his partner slips onto his lap backwards.

99

In Reverse

Instead of sitting on her lover's lap, the woman stands with her back to him while he is in the chair and holds up his legs while he enters her from behind, pulling her down onto him.

100

My Knight, My Chair

The man lies in a chair upside-down. His lover mounts him from above, resting her knees on the arms of the chair. He can hold her ankles for support, so he doesn't slip off. (He could get light-headed, so work quickly!)

101

Chair Twister

The man sits in a chair and the woman gets in the Hoover (87) in front of him, with her legs resting on either side of his face. Both partners win, but the games have just begun!

Checklist

This handy checklist is useful in many ways. Not only does it give you a thumbnail visual of each position for quick reference, but it also allows you to keep track of the positions as you enjoy them. Or, be creative and make icons for your favorite positons, easy positions, and positions that will take some yoga classes to master!

1 Straight-Edge Sex A

2 Foot Rub with Rhythm

3 Straight-Edge Sex B

4 Always by Your Side

5 Pig in a Blanket

6 The Penitent Forgiven

7 The Awakening

8 The Piked Awakening

9 Inner Awakening

10 Scissors

11 Splitting of a Bamboo

12 Hammerhead

13 Jackknifed Splits

14 Lateral Jackknifed Splits

15 Climbing Ivy

16 Inverted Wheelbarrow

17 The Crab

22 Side-to-Side Press

27 Lateral Kneel and Extend

32 Pelvic Lap Dance

18 The Wrapped Crab

23 Half Lotus

28 Kneel and Push Back

33 Locked Lap Dance

19 The Open Crab

24 Full Lotus

29 Side-to-Side Kneel and Extend

34 Kama's Wheel

20 The Press

25 Wife of Indra

30 Surf's Up

35 Reclining Kama's Wheel

21 The Bicycle

26 Kneel and Extend

31 Pelvic Thrust

36 Snake Trap

37 Full Reclining Snake Trap

42 Pair of Tongs

47 Stretched Spoon-on-Spoon

52 Will You Do Me?

38 The Neverending Hug

43 The Spinner

48 Sliding Into Home

53 Crouching Tiger, Hidden Passion

39 Paired Feet

44 Back to Meditating

49 The Recliner

54 Let Us Pray

40 "X" Marks the Spot

45 The Pin

50 The Wrap Around

55 The Body Hug

41 The Mare's Trick

46 Spoon-on-Spoon

51 The Bucking Bronco

56 Flexed Body Hug

57 Reclining Body Hug

62 Inverted Headlock

67 See Spot Come

72 Baby Elephant

58 Crying Out

63 The See-Saw A

68 The Dutch Doggy

73 Open Elephant

59 Sweet Abandon

64 The See-Saw B

69 Taking Sides

74 The Elephant

60 The Corkscrew

65 The Backbend A

70 The Back Scratcher

75 Sitting Body Wrap

61 The Flexed Corkscrew

66 The Throne

71 Enveloped in Love

76 Sitting Flexed Body Wrap

223

77 The Backbend B

82 Stand by Your Man

87 The Hoover

92 Purrfect Plunge

97 Tug of War

78 The Pushover

83 The Tango

88 The Hoover Upright

93 The Lounge Cat

98 Come Sit on My Lap

79 The Cobra

84 The Harness

89 The Handstand

94 Fido's on His Feet

99 In Reverse

80 The Pilot

85 The Backbend C

90 The Leg Up

95 The Wheelbarrow

100 My Knight, My Chair

81 The Stick Up

86 Congress of the Cow

91 The Chair Lift

96 Lay-Z Girl

101 Chair Twister